Alabama

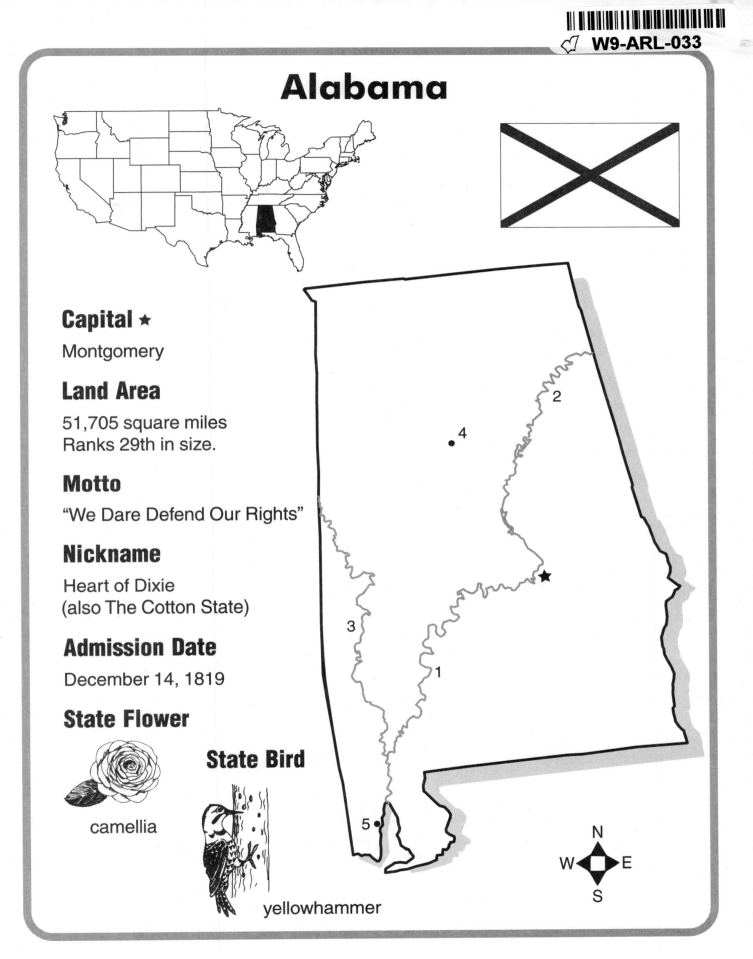

Capital ★

Montgomery

Land Area

51,705 square miles
Ranks 29th in size.

Motto

"We Dare Defend Our Rights"

Nickname

Heart of Dixie
(also The Cotton State)

Admission Date

December 14, 1819

State Flower

camellia

State Bird

yellowhammer

N
W E
S

Maps of the U.S.A 1-6 EMC 191

Alaska

Capital ★

Juneau

Land Area

591,009 square miles
Ranks first in size.

Nickname

The Last Frontier
(also Great Land)

Admission Date

January 3, 1959

Motto

"North to the Future"

State Flower

forget-me-not

State Bird

willow ptarmigan

Arizona

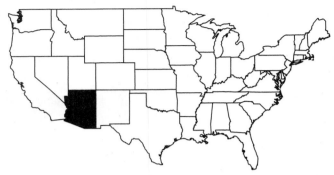

Capital ★

Phoenix

Land Area

114,000 square miles
Ranks sixth in size.

Motto

"God Enriches"

Nickname

Grand Canyon State

Admission Date

February 14, 1912

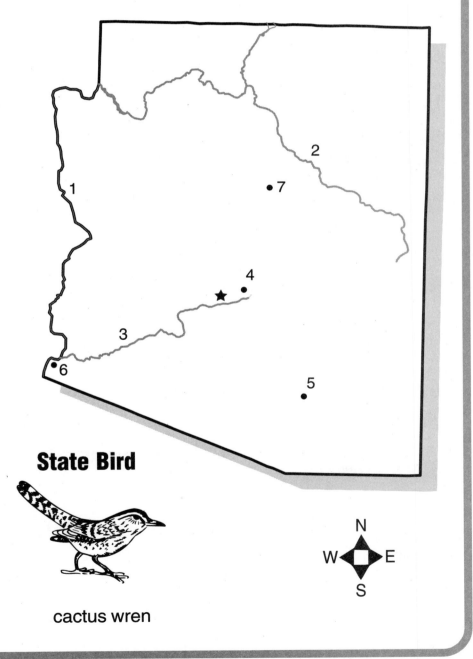

State Flower

saguaro blossom

State Bird

cactus wren

Arkansas

Capital ★

Little Rock

Land Area

53,187 square miles
Ranks 27th in size.

Motto

"The People Rule"

Nickname

Land of Opportunity
(also Razorback State)

Admission Date

June 15, 1836

State Flower

apple blossom

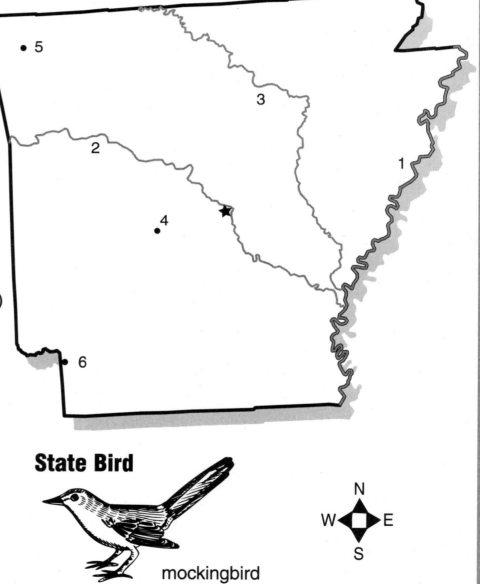

State Bird

mockingbird

California

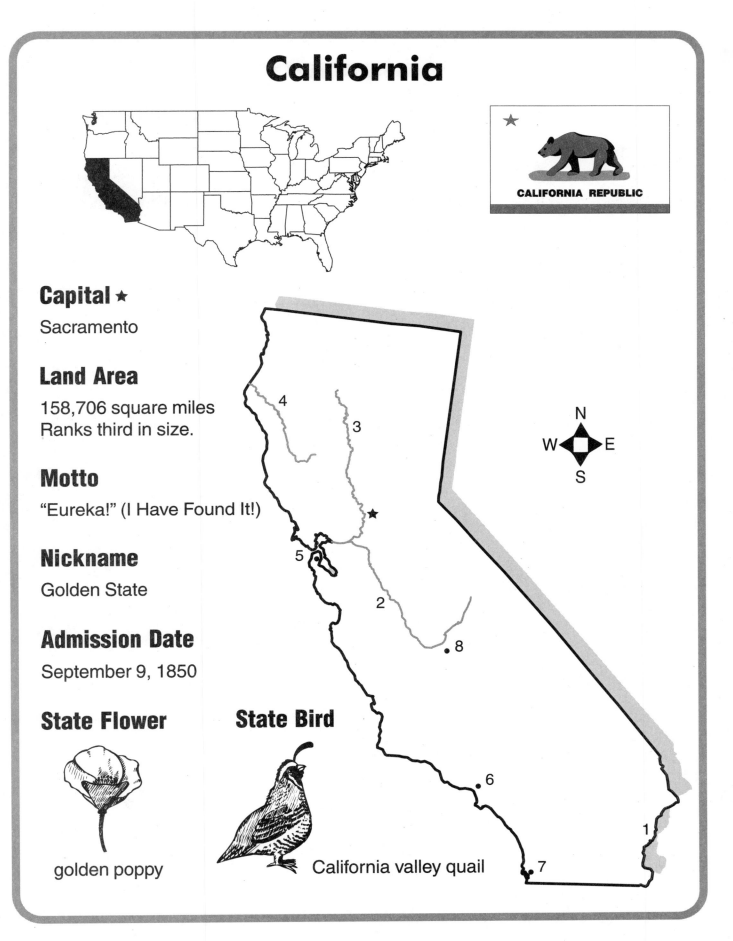

Capital ★

Sacramento

Land Area

158,706 square miles
Ranks third in size.

Motto

"Eureka!" (I Have Found It!)

Nickname

Golden State

Admission Date

September 9, 1850

State Flower

golden poppy

State Bird

California valley quail

CALIFORNIA REPUBLIC

Maps of the U.S.A 1-6 EMC 191

Colorado

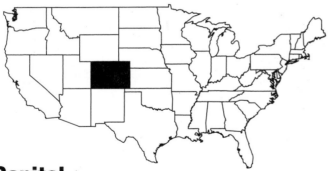

Capital ★

Denver

Land Area

104,091 square miles
Ranks eighth in size.

Motto

"Nothing Without Providence"

Nickname

Centennial State

Admission Date

August 1, 1876

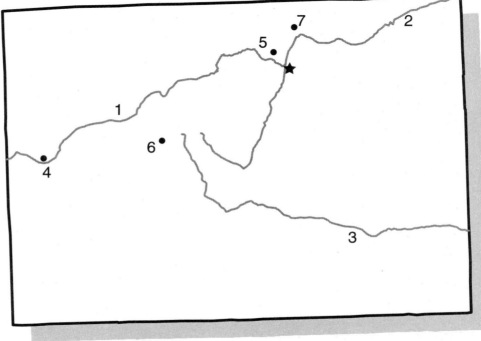

State Flower

blue columbine

State Bird

lark bunting

Maps of the U.S.A 1-6 EMC 191

Connecticut

Capital ★

Hartford

Nickname

The Nutmeg State
(also The Constitution State)

Admission Date

January 9, 1788
Fifth of the 13
original states.

Land Area

5,018 square miles
Ranks 48th in size.

Motto

"He Who Transplanted
Still Sustains"

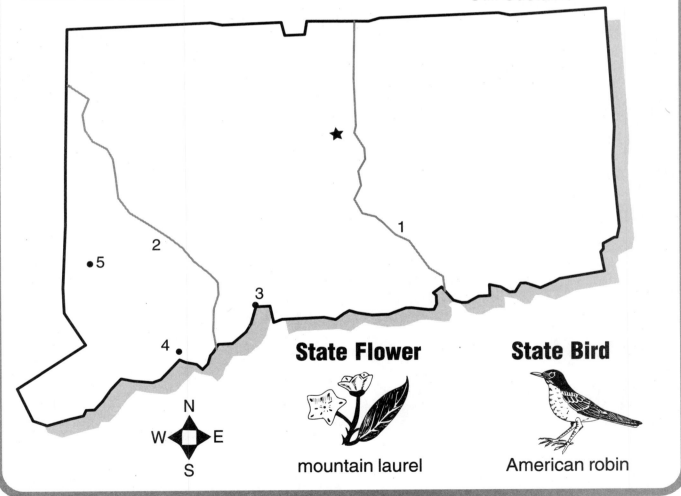

State Flower

mountain laurel

State Bird

American robin

Delaware

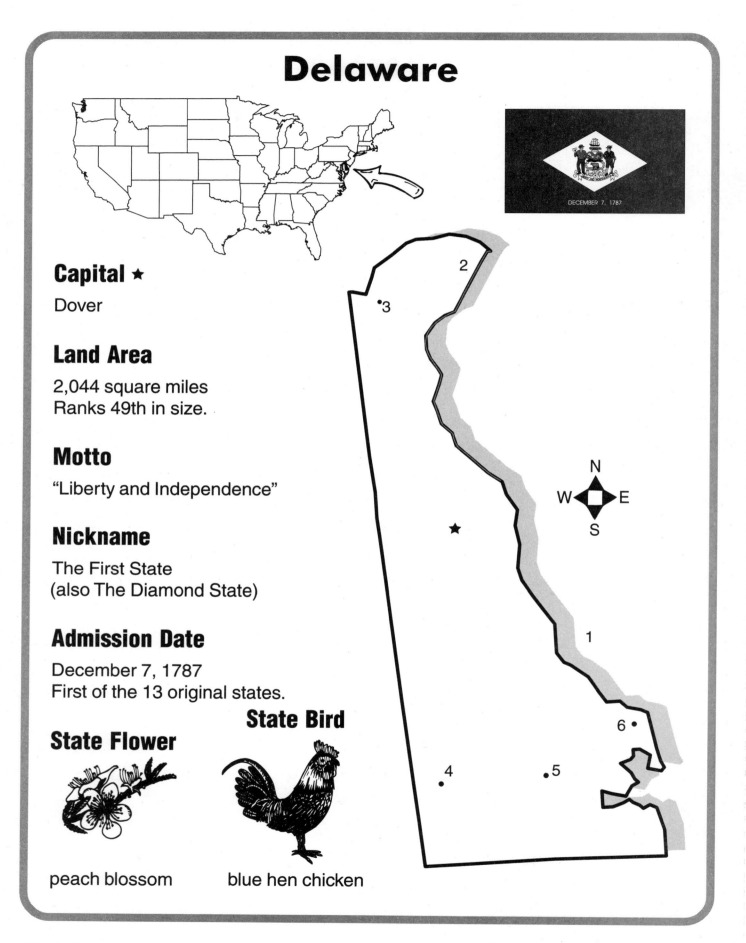

DECEMBER 7, 1787

Capital ★

Dover

Land Area

2,044 square miles
Ranks 49th in size.

Motto

"Liberty and Independence"

Nickname

The First State
(also The Diamond State)

Admission Date

December 7, 1787
First of the 13 original states.

State Flower

peach blossom

State Bird

blue hen chicken

Florida

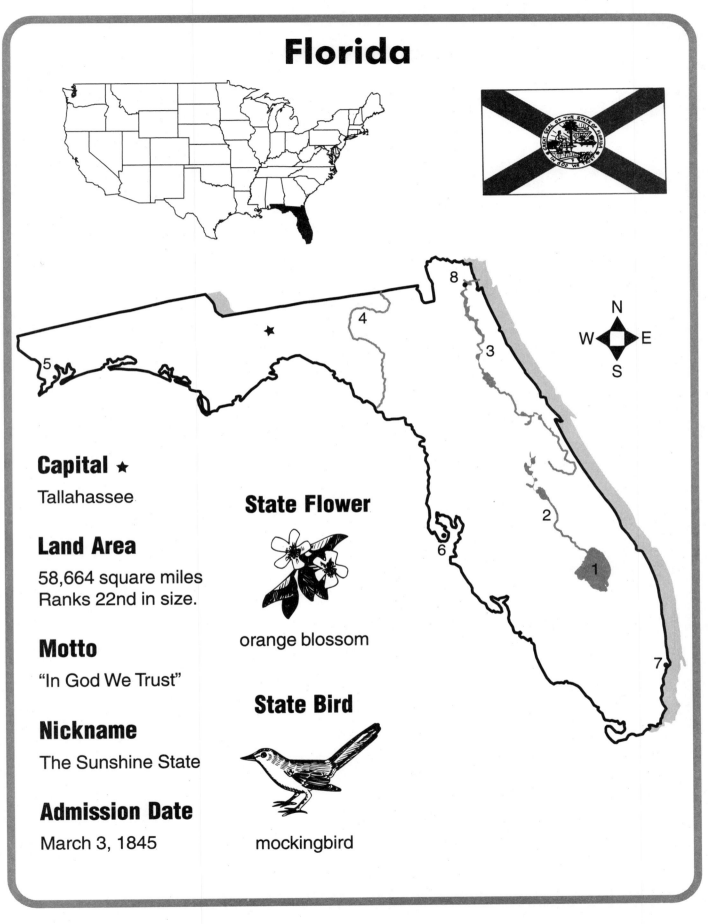

Capital ★

Tallahassee

Land Area

58,664 square miles
Ranks 22nd in size.

Motto

"In God We Trust"

Nickname

The Sunshine State

Admission Date

March 3, 1845

State Flower

orange blossom

State Bird

mockingbird

Maps of the U.S.A 1-6 EMC 191

Georgia

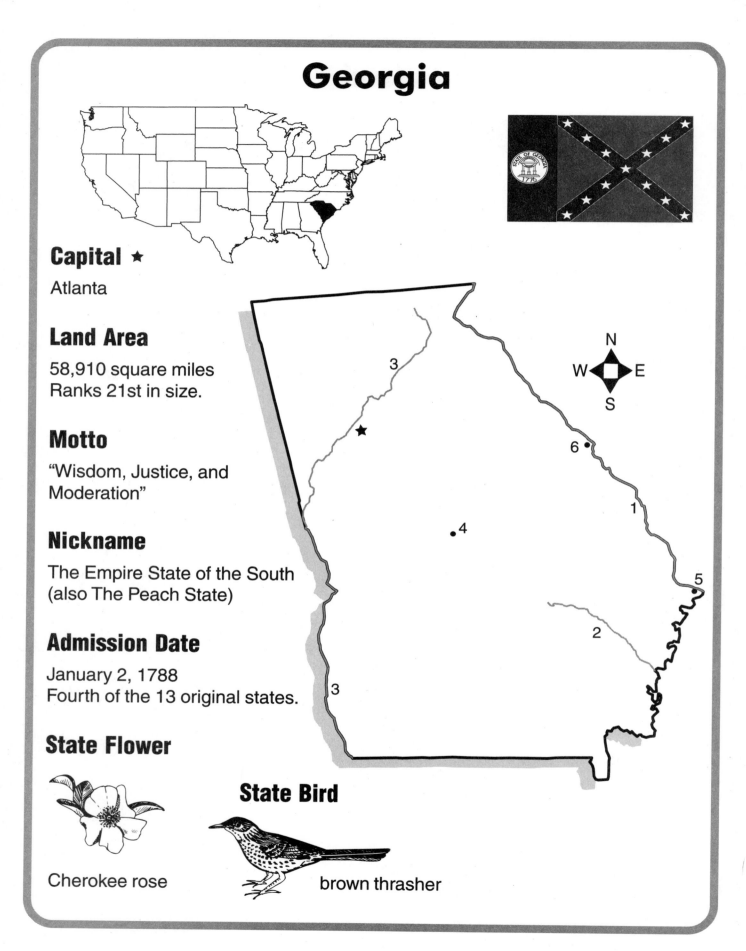

Capital ★

Atlanta

Land Area

58,910 square miles
Ranks 21st in size.

Motto

"Wisdom, Justice, and
Moderation"

Nickname

The Empire State of the South
(also The Peach State)

Admission Date

January 2, 1788
Fourth of the 13 original states.

State Flower

Cherokee rose

State Bird

brown thrasher

Maps of the U.S.A 1-6 EMC 191

Hawaii

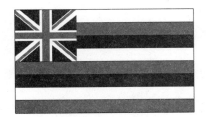

Capital ★

Honolulu

Motto

"The Life of the Land is Perpetuated in Righteousness"

Nickname

Aloha State

Land Area

6,471 square miles
Ranks 47th in size.

Admission Date

August 21, 1959

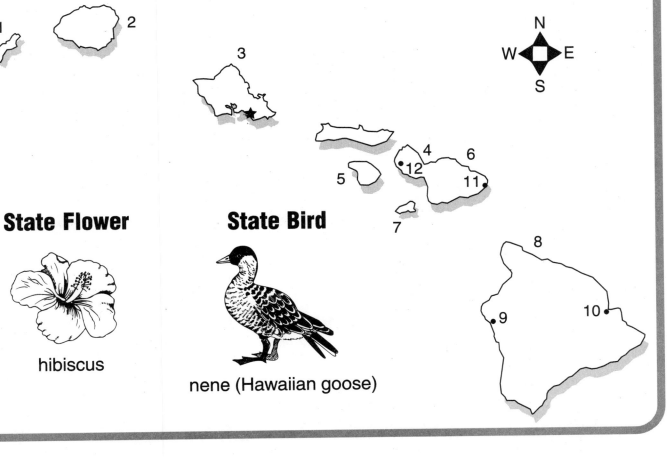

State Flower

hibiscus

State Bird

nene (Hawaiian goose)

Maps of the U.S.A 1-6 EMC 191

Idaho

Capital ★

Boise

Land Area

83,564 square miles
Ranks 13th in size.

Motto

"It is Perpetual"

Nickname

Gem State

Admission Date

July 3, 1890

State Flower

syringa (mock orange)

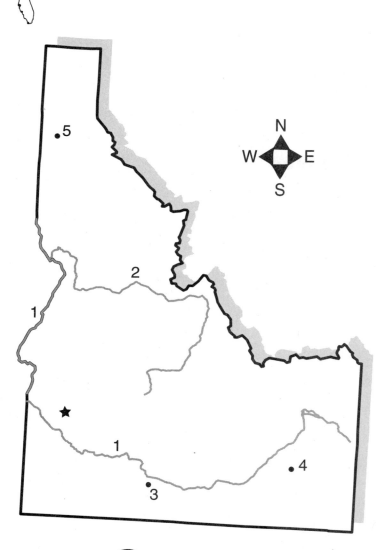

State Bird

mountain bluebird

Maps of the U.S.A 1-6 EMC 191

Illinois

ILLINOIS

Capital ★

Springfield

Land Area

56,345 square miles
Ranks 24th in size.

Motto

"State Sovereignty,
National Union"

Nickname

Land of Lincoln
(also Prairie State)

Admission Date

December 3, 1818

State Flower

Native Violet

State Bird

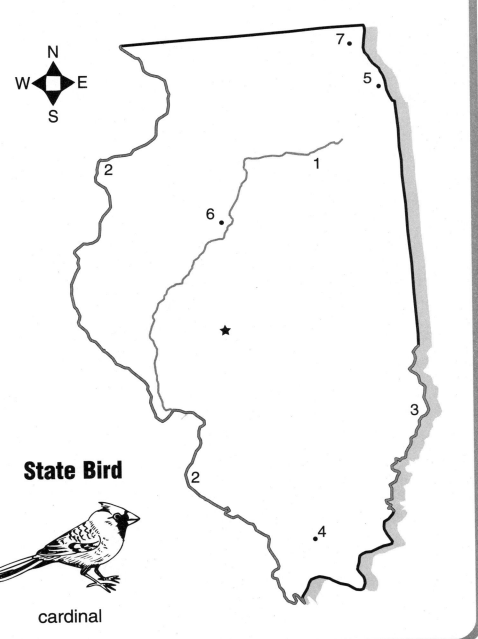

cardinal

Maps of the U.S.A 1-6 EMC 191

Indiana

Capital ★

Indianapolis

Land Area

36,185 square miles
Ranks 38th in size.

Motto

"The Crossroads of America"

Nickname

Hoosier State

Admission Date

December 11, 1816

State Flower   State Bird

peony   cardinal

Iowa

IOWA

Capital ★

Des Moines

Land Area

56,275 square miles
Ranks 25th in size.

Motto

"Our Liberties We Prize and
Our Rights We Will Maintain"

Nickname

The Hawkeye State

Admission Date

December 28, 1846

State Flower

wild rose

State Bird

goldfinch

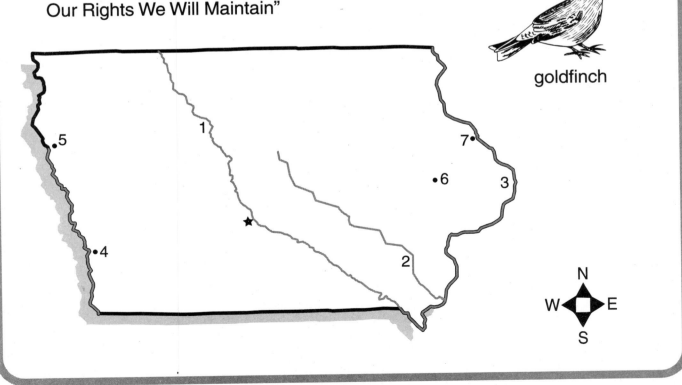

Maps of the U.S.A 1-6 EMC 191

Kansas

Capital ★

Topeka

Land Area

82,277 square miles
Ranks 14th in size.

Motto

"To the Stars
Through Difficulties"

Nickname

Sunflower State
(also Jayhawk State)

Admission Date

January 29, 1861

State Flower

sunflower

State Bird

western
meadowlark

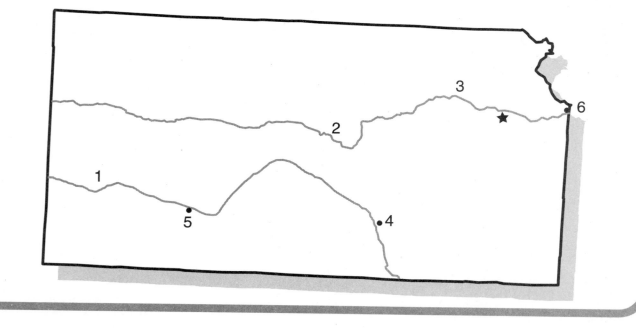

Maps of the U.S.A 1-6 EMC 191

Kentucky

Capital ★

Frankfort

Land Area

40,409 square miles
Ranks 37th in size.

Motto

"United We Stand,
Divided We Fall"

Nickname

The Bluegrass State

Admission Date

June 1, 1792

State Flower

goldenrod

State Bird

cardinal

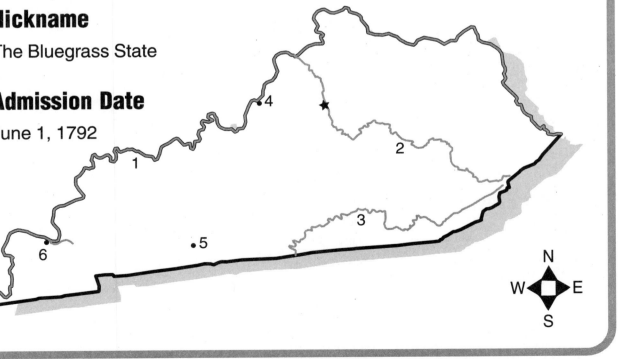

Maps of the U.S.A 1-6 EMC 191

Louisiana

Capital ★

Baton Rouge

Land Area

47,752 square
miles
Ranks 31st in size.

Motto

"Union, Justice
and Confidence"

Nickname

The Pelican State
(also The Creole State)

Admission Date

April 30, 1812

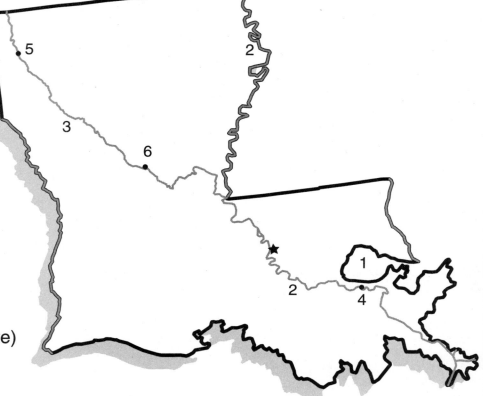

State Flower

magnolia

State Bird

eastern brown pelican

Maine

Capital ★

Augusta

Land Area

33,265 square miles
Ranks 39th in size.

Motto

"I Direct"

Nickname

The Pine Tree State

Admission Date

March 15, 1820

State Flower

white pine cone
and tassel

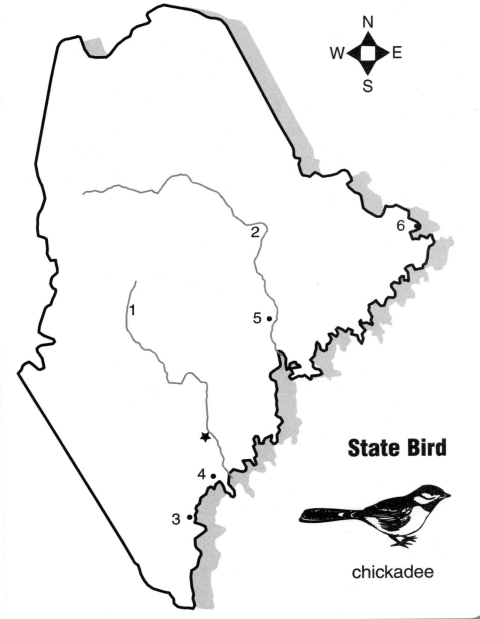

State Bird

chickadee

Maryland

Capital ★

Annapolis

Land Area

10,460 square miles
Ranks 42nd in size.

Motto

"Manly Deeds,
Womanly Words"

Nickname

The Old Line State
(also Free State, Pine Tree
State, Lumber State)

Admission Date

April 28, 1788
Seventh of the
13 original states.

State Flower

black-eyed
susan

State Bird

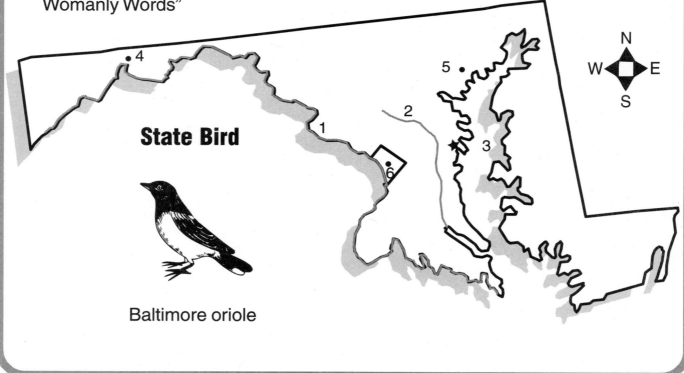

Baltimore oriole

Massachusetts

Capital ★

Boston

Land Area

8,284 square miles
Ranks 45th in size.

Motto

"By the Sword We Seek Peace,
but Peace Only Under Liberty"

Nickname

The Bay State
(also The Old Colony
State)

Admission Date

February 6, 1788
Sixth of the 13
original states.

State Flower

mayflower (arbutus)

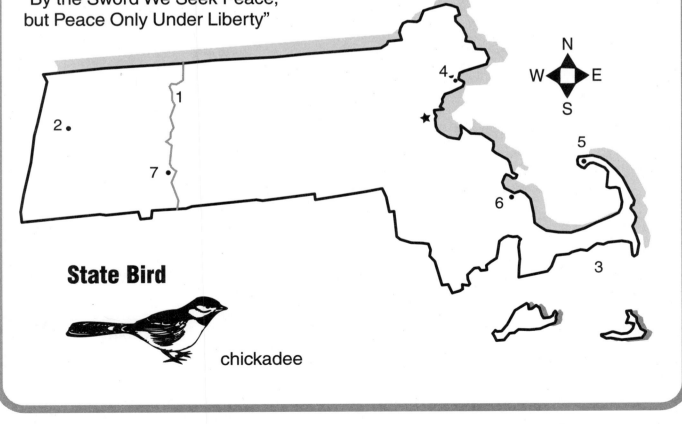

State Bird

chickadee

Michigan

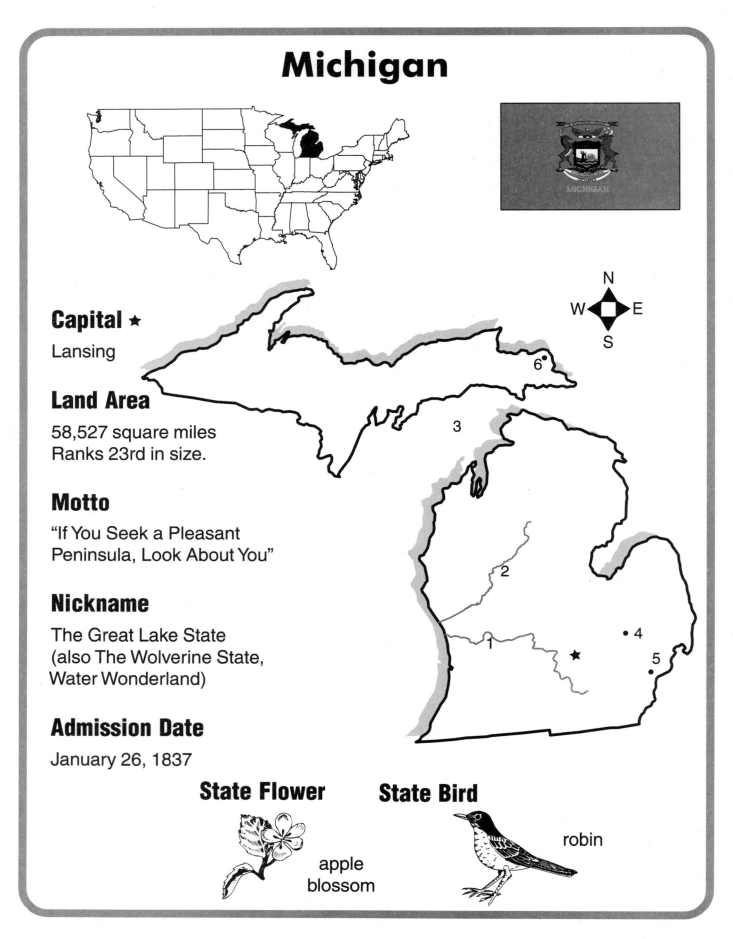

Capital ★

Lansing

Land Area

58,527 square miles
Ranks 23rd in size.

Motto

"If You Seek a Pleasant
Peninsula, Look About You"

Nickname

The Great Lake State
(also The Wolverine State,
Water Wonderland)

Admission Date

January 26, 1837

State Flower

apple blossom

State Bird

robin

Minnesota

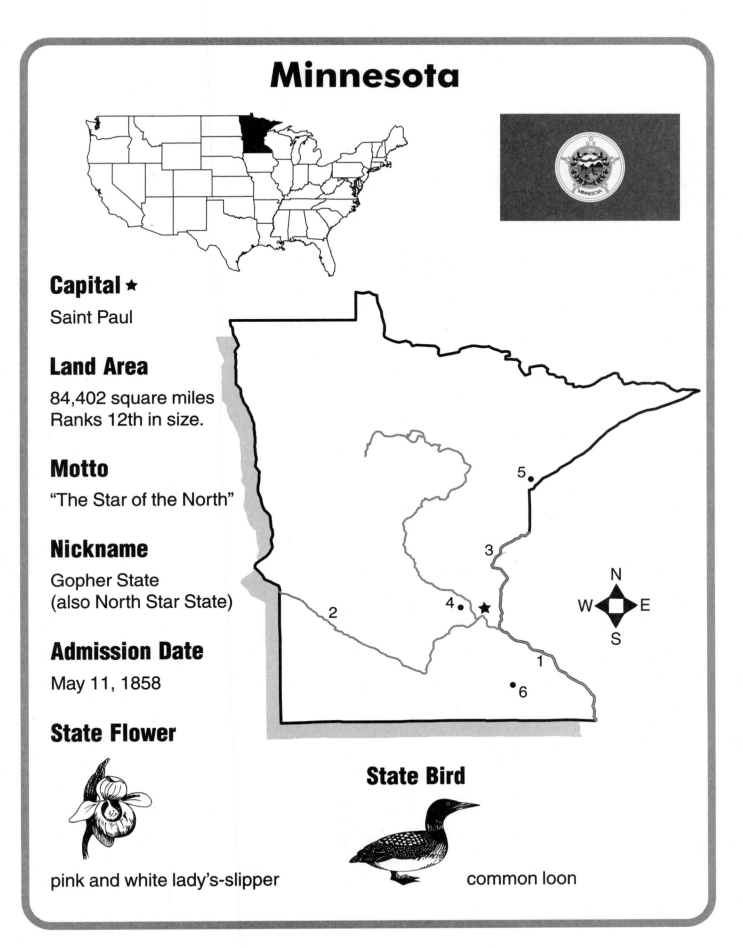

Capital ★
Saint Paul

Land Area
84,402 square miles
Ranks 12th in size.

Motto
"The Star of the North"

Nickname
Gopher State
(also North Star State)

Admission Date
May 11, 1858

State Flower
pink and white lady's-slipper

State Bird
common loon

Maps of the U.S.A 1-6 EMC 191

Mississippi

Capital ★

Jackson

Land Area

47,689 square miles
Ranks 32nd in size.

Motto

"By Valor and Arms"

Nickname

The Magnolia State

Admission Date

December 10, 1817

State Flower

magnolia

State Bird

mockingbird

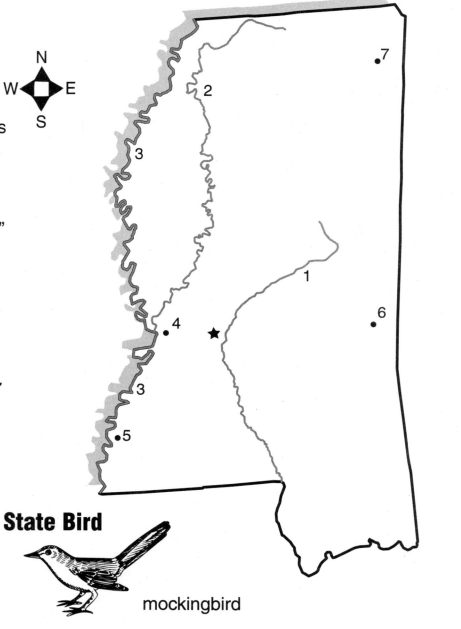

Missouri

Capital ★

Jefferson City

Land Area

69,697 square miles
Ranks 19th in size.

Motto

"The Welfare of the People
Shall Be the Supreme Law"

Nickname

The Show Me State

Admission Date

August 10, 1821

State Flower

hawthorn

State Bird

eastern
bluebird

Montana

Capital ★

Helena

Land Area

147,046 square miles
Ranks 4th in size.

Motto

"Gold and Silver"

Nickname

Treasure State

Admission Date

Nov. 8, 1889

State Flower

bitterroot

State Bird

western meadowlark

Nebraska

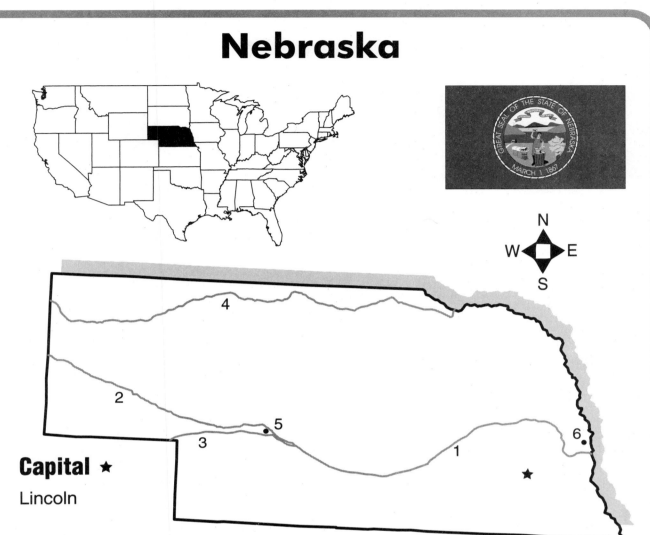

Capital ★

Lincoln

Land Area

77,355 square miles
Ranks 15th in size.

Motto

"Equality Before the Law"

Nickname

Cornhusker State
(also Tree Planters State)

Admission Date

March 1, 1867

State Flower

goldenrod

State Bird

western meadowlark

Nevada

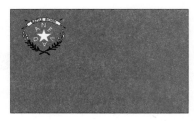

Capital ★

Carson City

Land Area

110,561 square miles
Ranks seventh in size.

Motto

"All for Our Country"

Nickname

Sagebrush State
(also Silver State, Battle
Born State)

Admission Date

October 31, 1864

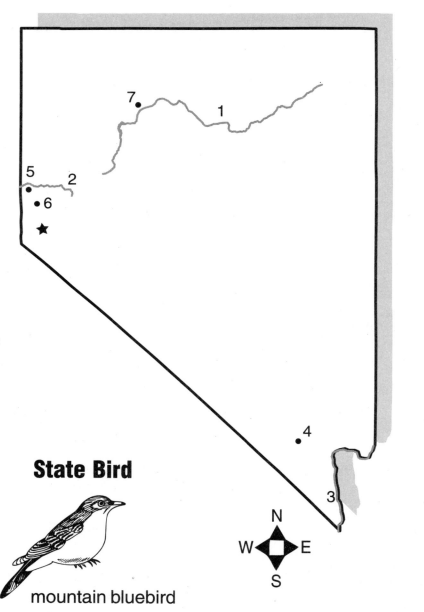

State Flower

sagebrush

State Bird

mountain bluebird

New Hampshire

Capital ★

Concord

Land Area

9,279 square miles
Ranks 44th in size.

Motto

"Live Free or Die"

Nickname

The Granite State

Admission Date

June 21, 1788
Ninth of the 13
original states.

State Flower

purple lilac

State Bird

purple finch

New Jersey

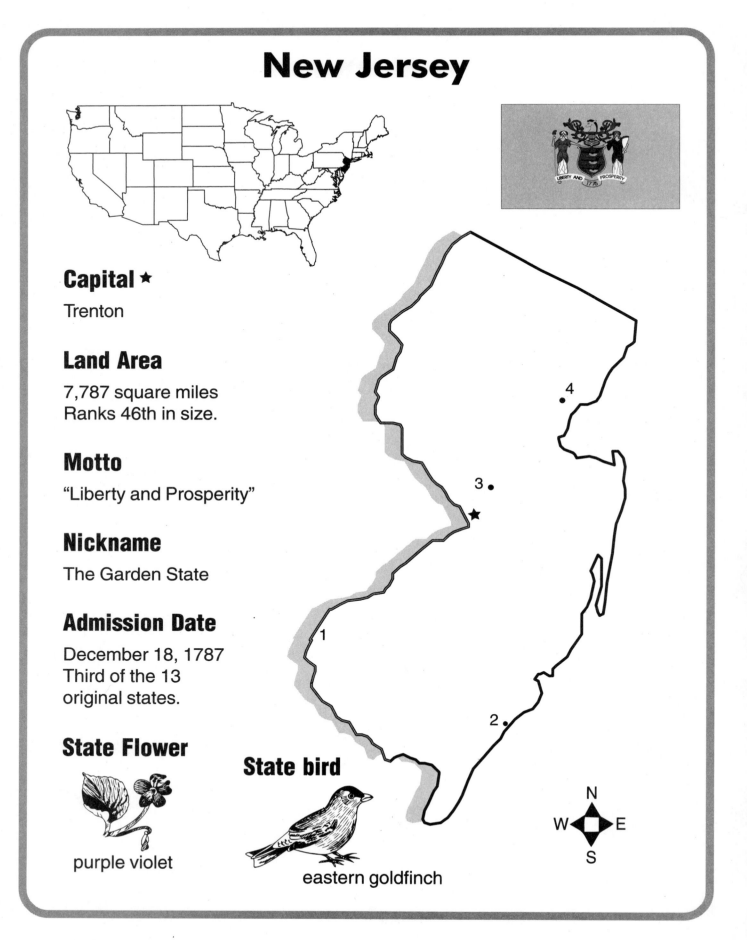

Capital ★

Trenton

Land Area

7,787 square miles
Ranks 46th in size.

Motto

"Liberty and Prosperity"

Nickname

The Garden State

Admission Date

December 18, 1787
Third of the 13
original states.

State Flower

purple violet

State bird

eastern goldfinch

Maps of the U.S.A 1-6 EMC 191

New Mexico

Capital ★

Santa Fe

Land Area

121,593 square miles
Ranks fifth in size.

Motto

"It Grows as It Goes"

Nickname

Land of Enchantment

Admission Date

January 6, 1912

State Flower

yucca

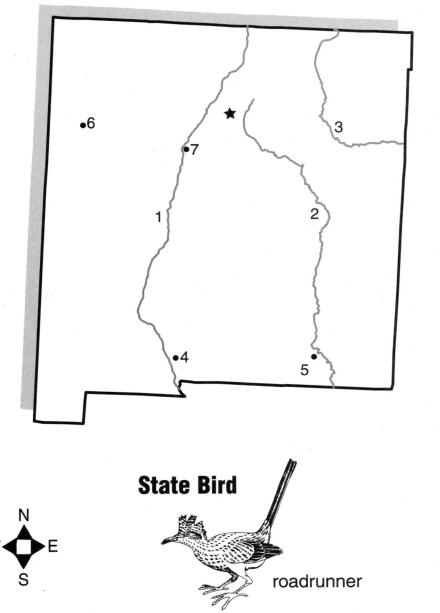

N
W ◆ E
S

State Bird

roadrunner

New York

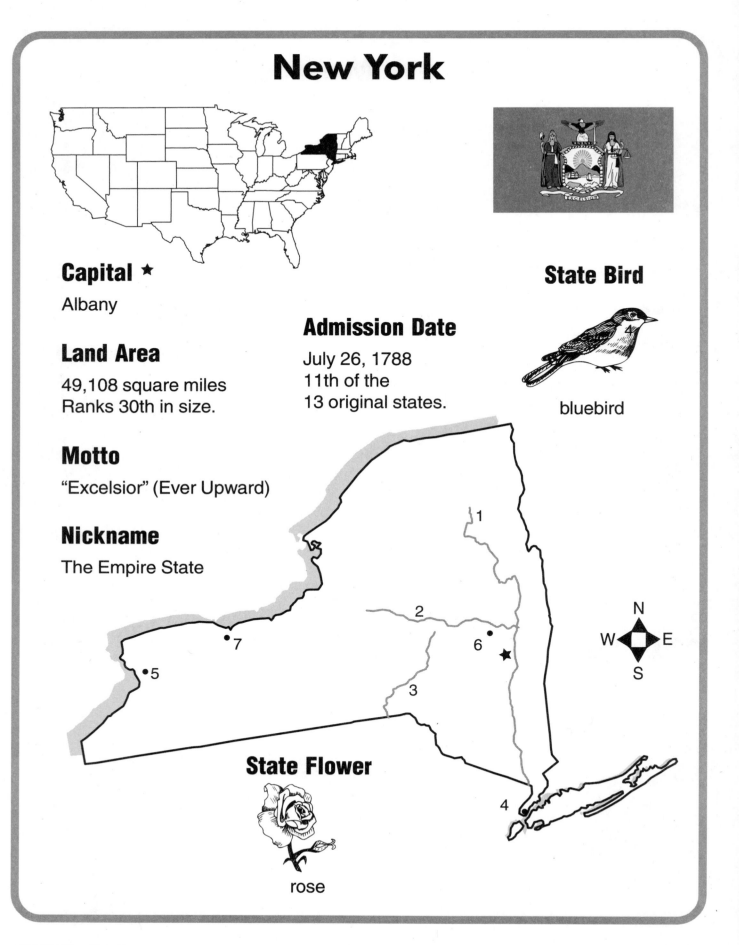

Capital ★

Albany

Land Area

49,108 square miles
Ranks 30th in size.

Motto

"Excelsior" (Ever Upward)

Nickname

The Empire State

Admission Date

July 26, 1788
11th of the
13 original states.

State Bird

bluebird

State Flower

rose

North Carolina

Capital ★

Raleigh

Land Area

52,669 square miles
Ranks 28th in size.

Motto

"To Be, Rather
Than to Seem"

Nickname

The Tar Heel State
(also Old North State)

Admission Date

November 21, 1789
12th of the 13 original states.

State Bird

cardinal

State Flower

dogwood

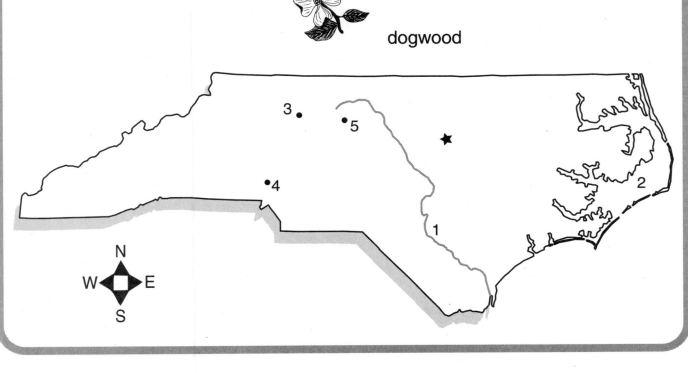

North Dakota

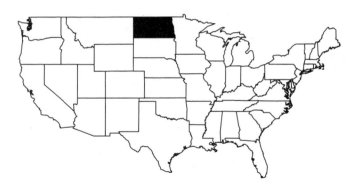

Capital ★

Bismarck

Land Area

70,702 square miles
Ranks 17th in size.

Motto

"Liberty and Union,
Now and Forever,
One and Inseparable"

Nickname

Peace Garden State
(also Sioux State)

Admission Date

Nov. 2, 1889

State Flower

wild prairie rose

State Bird

western meadowlark

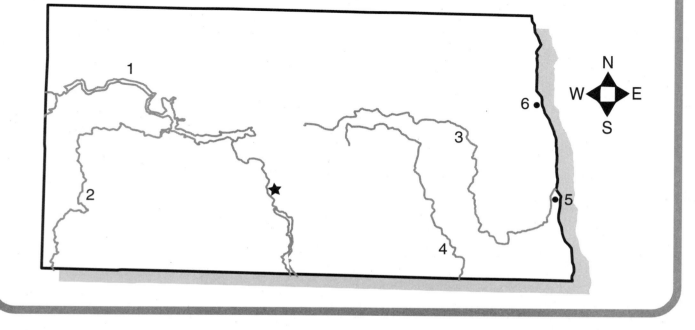

Ohio

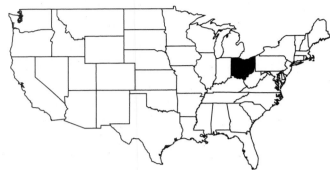

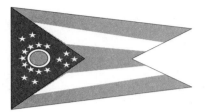

Capital ★
Columbus

Land Area
41,330 square miles
Ranks 35th in size.

Motto
"With God, All Things
Are Possible"

Nickname
The Buckeye State

Admission Date
March 1, 1803

State Flower

scarlet carnation

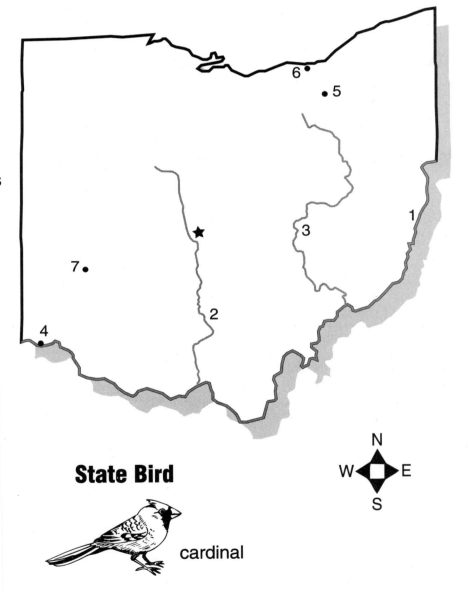

State Bird

cardinal

Oklahoma

Capital ★

Oklahoma City

Area

69,956 square miles
Ranks 18th in size.

Motto

"Labor Conquers All Things"

Nickname

Sooner State

Admission Date

November 16, 1907

State Bird

scissor-tailed
flycatcher

State Flower

mistletoe

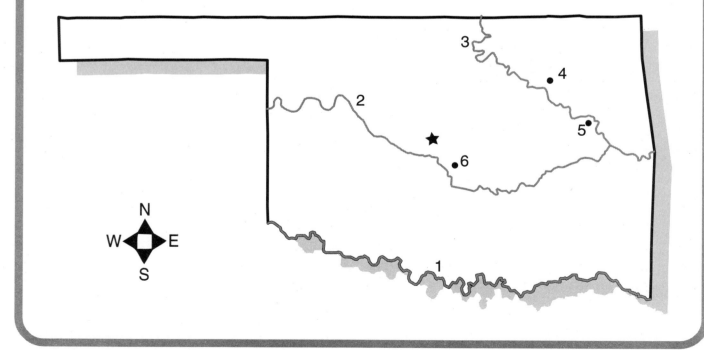

Oregon

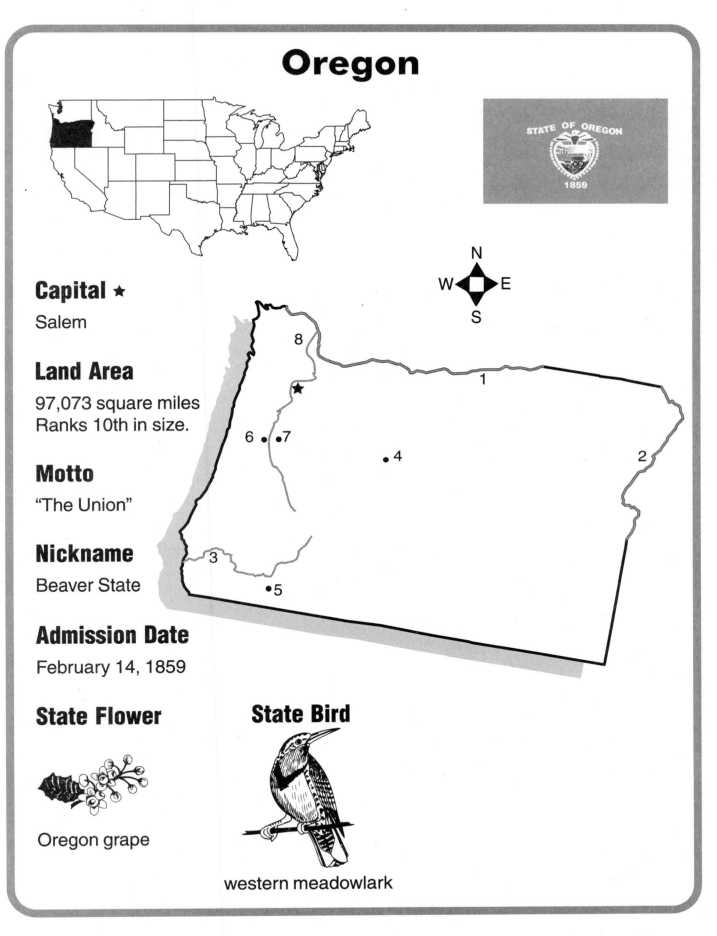

Capital ★

Salem

Land Area

97,073 square miles
Ranks 10th in size.

Motto

"The Union"

Nickname

Beaver State

Admission Date

February 14, 1859

State Flower

Oregon grape

State Bird

western meadowlark

Pennsylvania

Capital ★

Harrisburg

Land Area

45,308 square miles
Ranks 33rd in size.

Motto

"Virtue, Liberty
and Independence"

Nickname

The Keystone State

Admission Date

December 12, 1787
Second of the 13
original states.

State Flower

mountain
laurel

State Bird

ruffed grouse

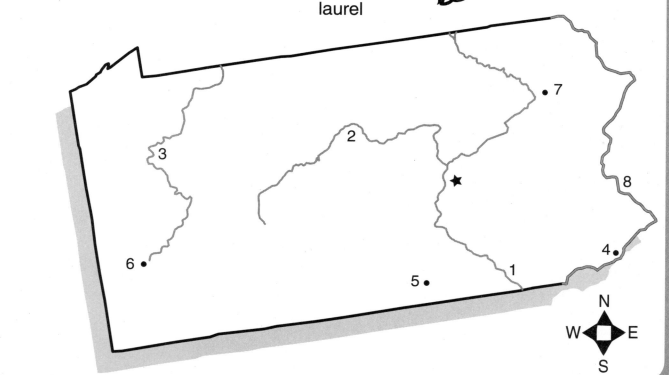

Rhode Island

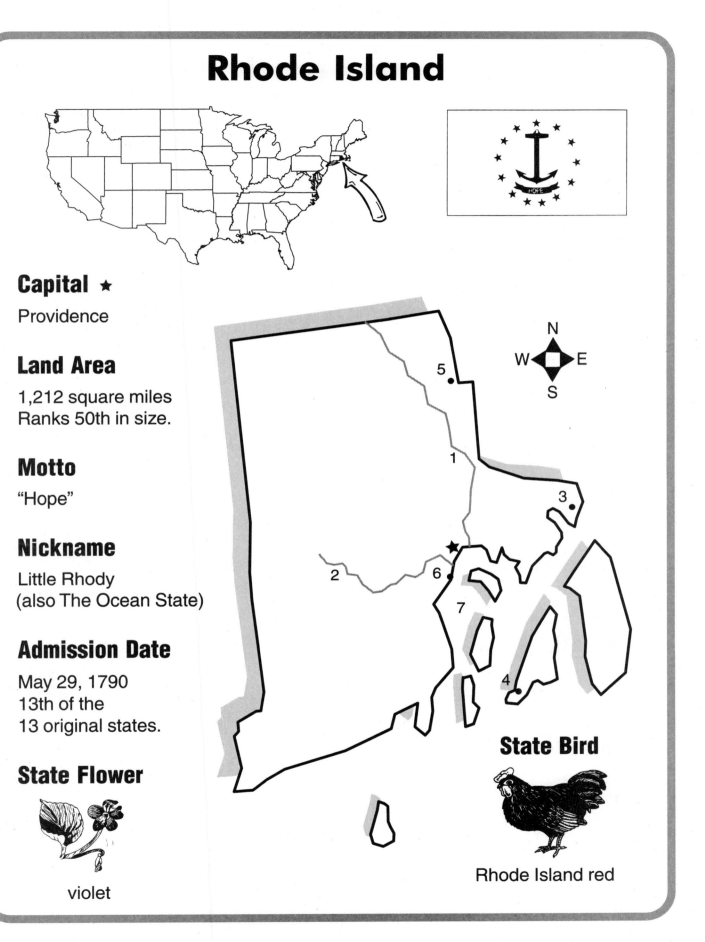

Capital ★

Providence

Land Area

1,212 square miles
Ranks 50th in size.

Motto

"Hope"

Nickname

Little Rhody
(also The Ocean State)

Admission Date

May 29, 1790
13th of the
13 original states.

State Flower

violet

State Bird

Rhode Island red

Maps of the U.S.A 1-6 EMC 191

South Carolina

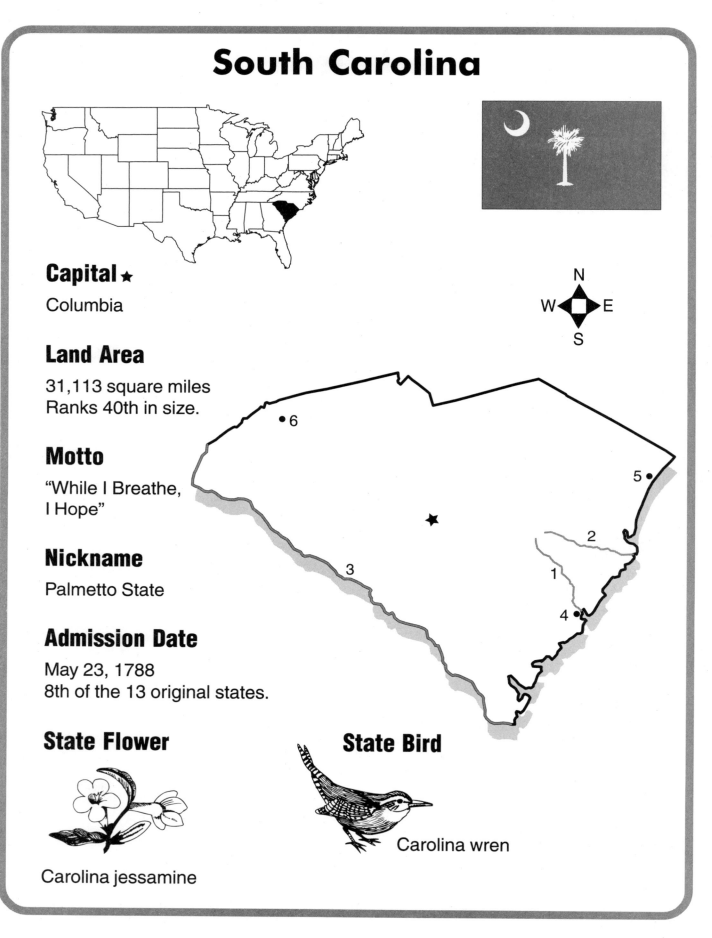

Capital ★

Columbia

Land Area

31,113 square miles
Ranks 40th in size.

Motto

"While I Breathe,
I Hope"

Nickname

Palmetto State

Admission Date

May 23, 1788
8th of the 13 original states.

State Flower

Carolina jessamine

State Bird

Carolina wren

South Dakota

State Flower

pasque flower

Capital ★

Pierre

Land Area

77,116 square miles
Ranks 16th in size.

Motto

"Under God the
People Rule"

Nickname

Sunshine State
(also Coyote State)

Admission Date

Nov. 2, 1889

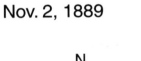

State Bird

ring-necked pheasant

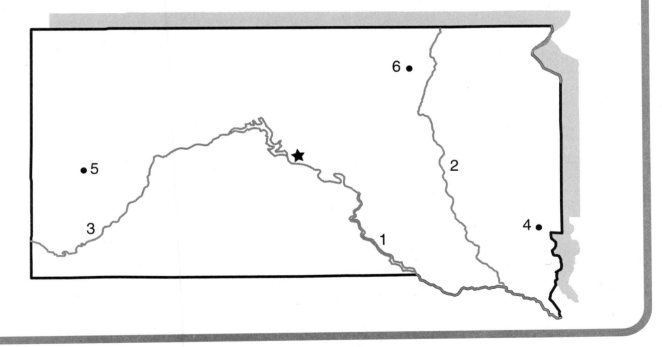

Tennessee

Capital ★

Nashville

Land Area

42,144 square miles
Ranks 34th in size.

Motto

"Agriculture and Commerce"
"Tennessee—America at
Its Best"

Nickname

The Volunteer State

Admission Date

June 1, 1796

State Flower

iris

State Bird

mockingbird

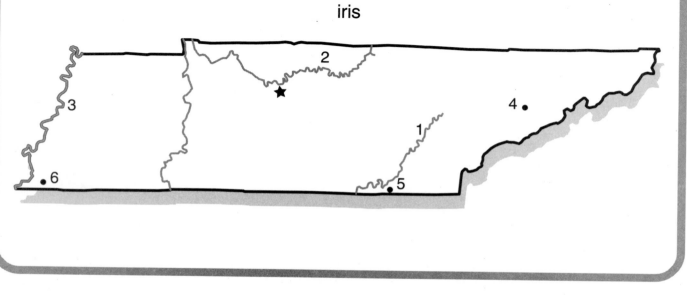

Maps of the U.S.A 1-6 EMC 191

Texas

Capital ★

Austin

Land Area

266,807 square miles
Ranks second in size.

Motto

"Friendship"

Nickname

Lone Star State

Admission Date

December 29, 1845

State Flower

bluebonnet

State Bird

mockingbird

Maps of the U.S.A 1-6 EMC 191

Utah

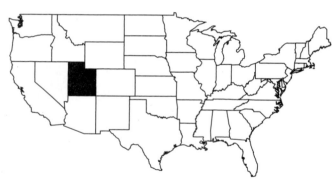

Capital ★

Salt Lake City

Land Area

84,899 square miles
Ranks 11th in size.

Motto

"Industry"

Nickname

Beehive State

Admission Date

January 4, 1896

State Flower

sego lily

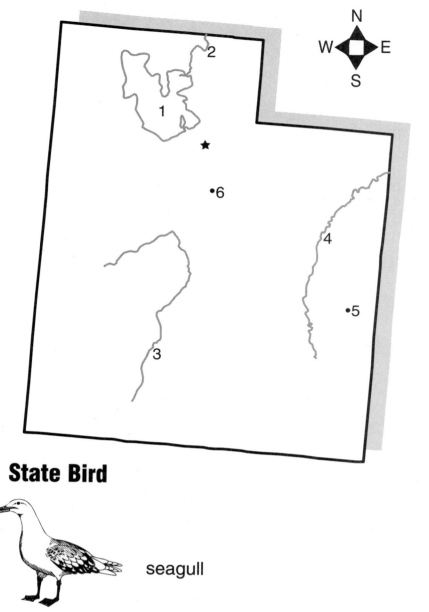

State Bird

seagull

Vermont

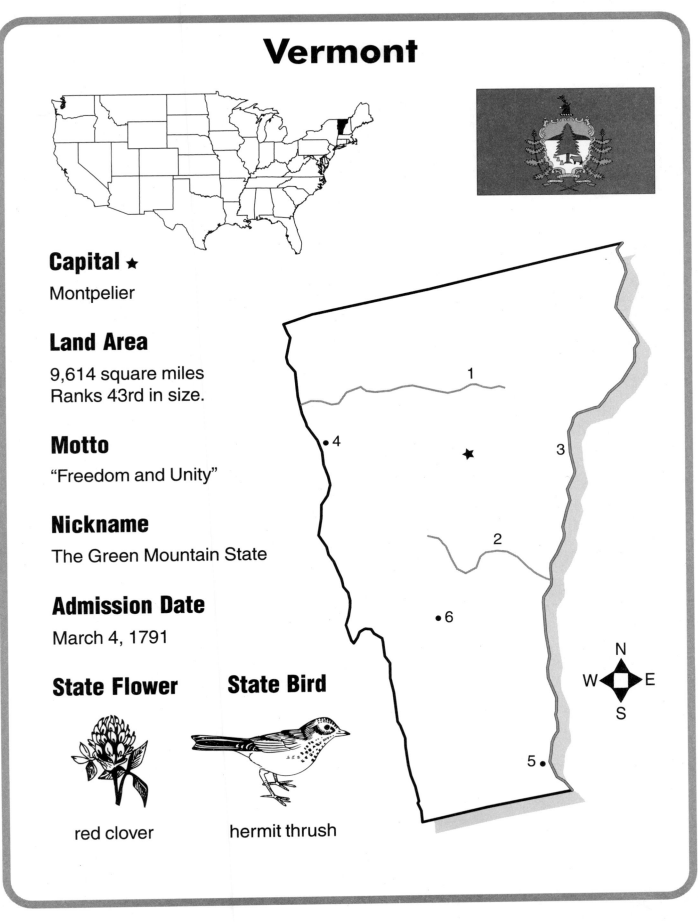

Capital ★

Montpelier

Land Area

9,614 square miles
Ranks 43rd in size.

Motto

"Freedom and Unity"

Nickname

The Green Mountain State

Admission Date

March 4, 1791

State Flower

red clover

State Bird

hermit thrush

Maps of the U.S.A 1-6 EMC 191

Virginia

Capital ★

Richmond

Land Area

40,767 square miles
Ranks 36th in size.

Motto

"Thus Always to Tyrants"

Nickname

The Old Dominion—
Mother of Presidents

Admission Date

June 25, 1788
10th of the 13 original states.

State Flower

dogwood

State Bird

cardinal

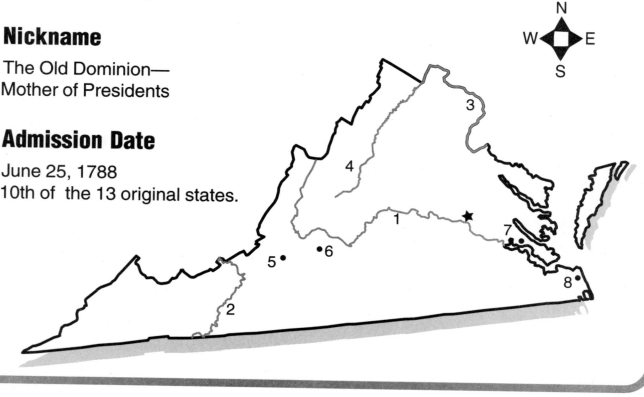

Maps of the U.S.A 1-6 EMC 191

Washington

State Capital ★

Olympia

Land Area

68,139 square miles
Ranks 20th size.

Motto

"By and By"

Nickname

Evergreen State

Admission date

November 11, 1889

State Flower

rhododendron

State Bird

willow goldfinch

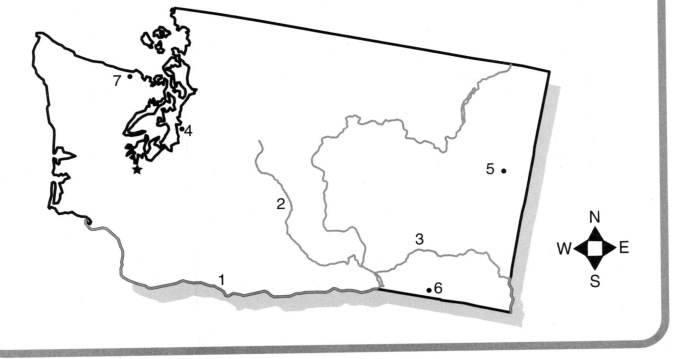

Maps of the U.S.A 1-6 EMC 191

West Virginia

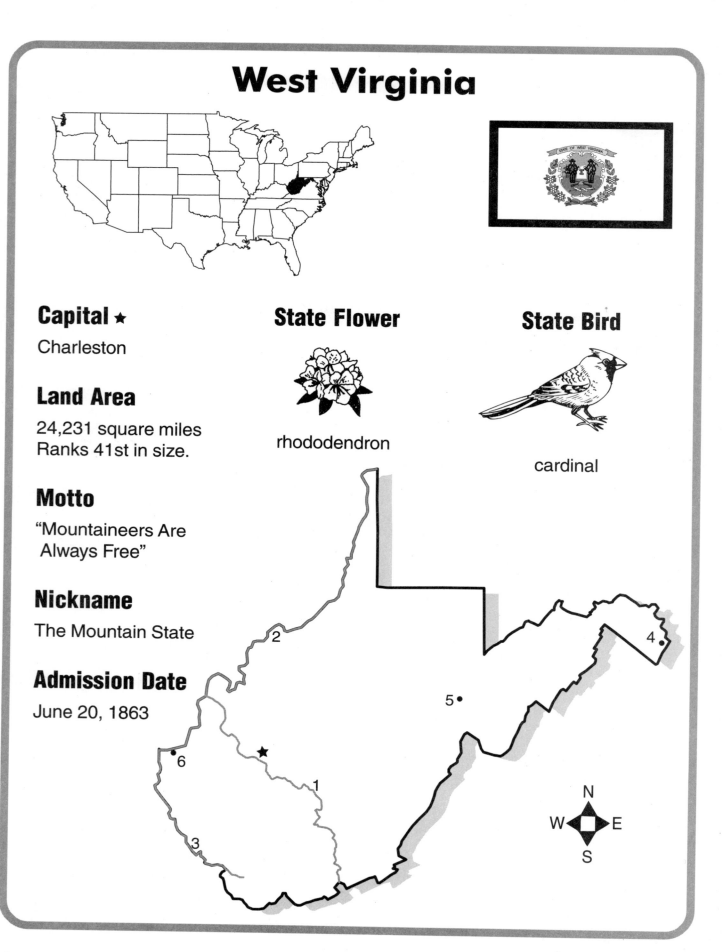

Capital ★

Charleston

Land Area

24,231 square miles
Ranks 41st in size.

Motto

"Mountaineers Are
 Always Free"

Nickname

The Mountain State

Admission Date

June 20, 1863

State Flower

rhododendron

State Bird

cardinal

Maps of the U.S.A 1-6 EMC 191

Wisconsin

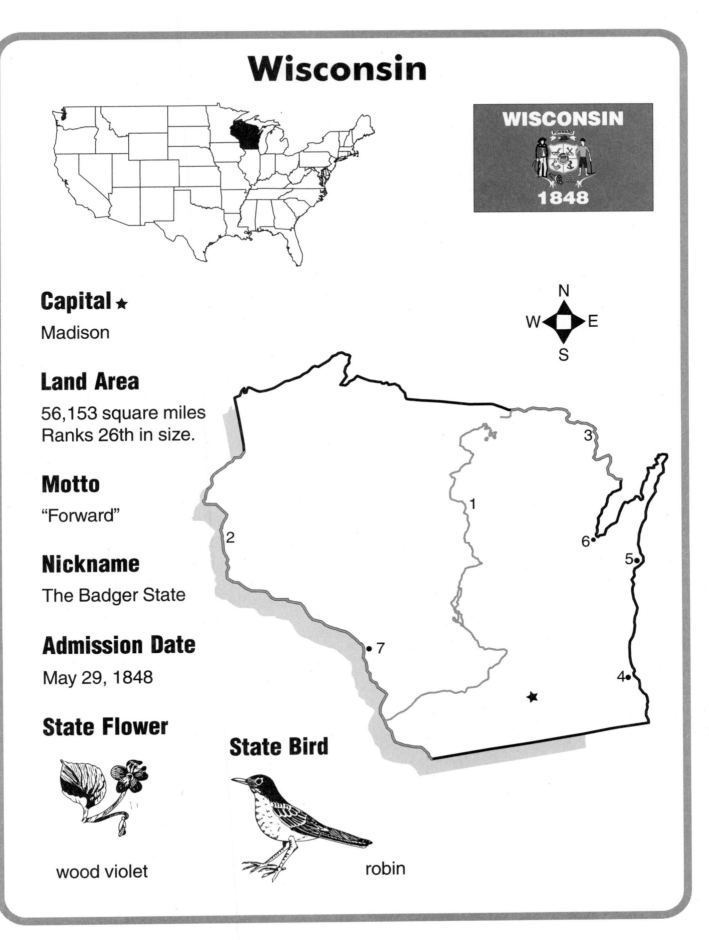

WISCONSIN
1848

Capital ★

Madison

Land Area

56,153 square miles
Ranks 26th in size.

Motto

"Forward"

Nickname

The Badger State

Admission Date

May 29, 1848

State Flower

wood violet

State Bird

robin

Maps of the U.S.A 1-6 EMC 191

Wyoming

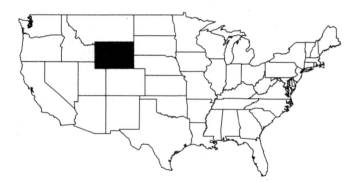

Capital ★
Cheyenne

Area
97,809 square miles
Ranks 9th in size.

Motto
"Equal Rights"

Nickname
Equality State

Admission Date
July 10, 1890

State Flower

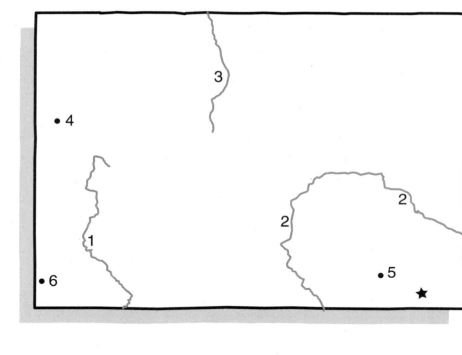

Indian paintbrush

State Bird

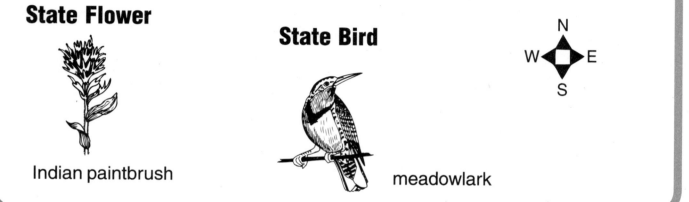

meadowlark

My Personal Geography

My state: _____   My city or town: _____

State capital: _____   My street: _____

                                            My zip code: _____

	Yes	No	Name
I live near an ocean.	_____	_____	_____
I live near a mountain.	_____	_____	_____
I live near a lake.	_____	_____	_____
I live in the country.	_____	_____	_____
I live in the city.	_____	_____	_____

Facts I Learned About My Town

Population: _____   Elevation: _____

Facts About My State

Motto: _____

_____

Nickname: _____

State flower: _____

Admission date: _____

State bird: _____

A picture of my state map.

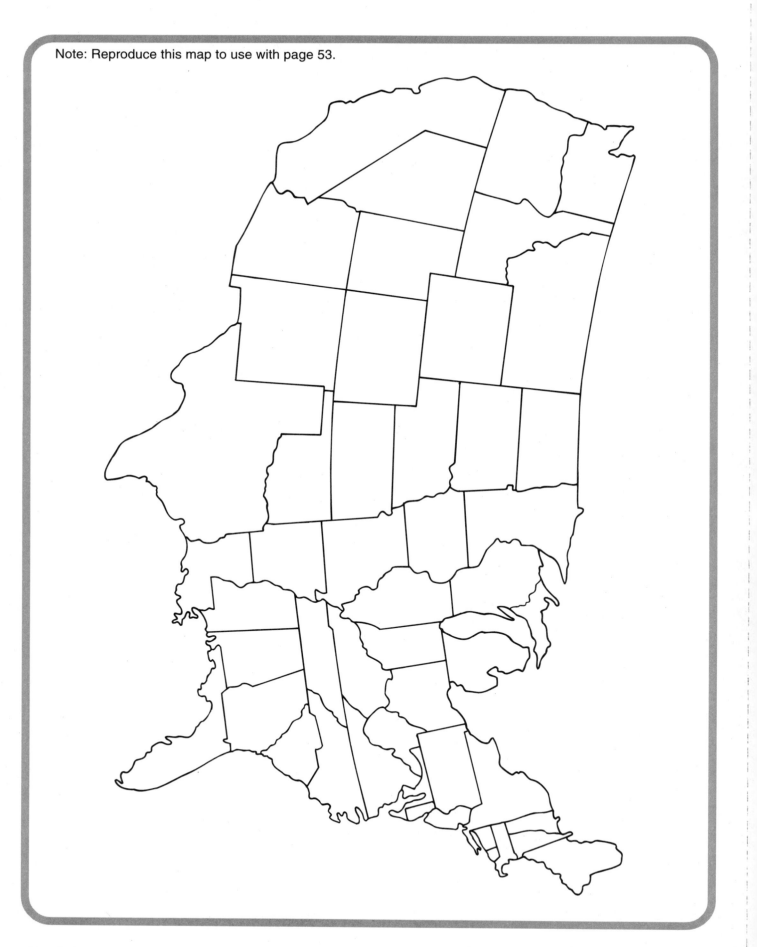

Maps of the U.S.A 1-6 EMC 191

Note: Use the map on page 52 with these activities.

Using the Blank Map of the United States of America

A Specific State

Have students label the state (or states) you are studying. Have students color in a selected state.

Ask questions such as:

1. Name all of the states that touch this state.

2. Which state is to the north (west, east, south) of the state?

3. Which states will you pass through if you travel from <u>(the state in which you live)</u> to <u>(name a state)</u>?

4. Which direction would you go to get from <u>(home state)</u> to <u>(name a state)</u>?

The Complete Map

1. Have students fill in the names of all the states. Write the names of smaller states, such as Rhode Island, in the margins and draw lines from the names to the correct area on the map.

   Ask questions such as:

   a. How many states are in the United States?

   b. Which two states are separate from the rest of the states?

   c. Which state is made up of islands? Which direction would you travel to reach this state?

2. Use the map to make a tally of the states in which your students were born. Turn this information into a graph.

3. Give students copies of the map. Have them color and label states in which they have lived or visited.

Challenges

These challenges can be done orally or in written form.

1. Name all of the states in the United States.

2. Locate each state on a blank map.

3. Give the capital of each state.

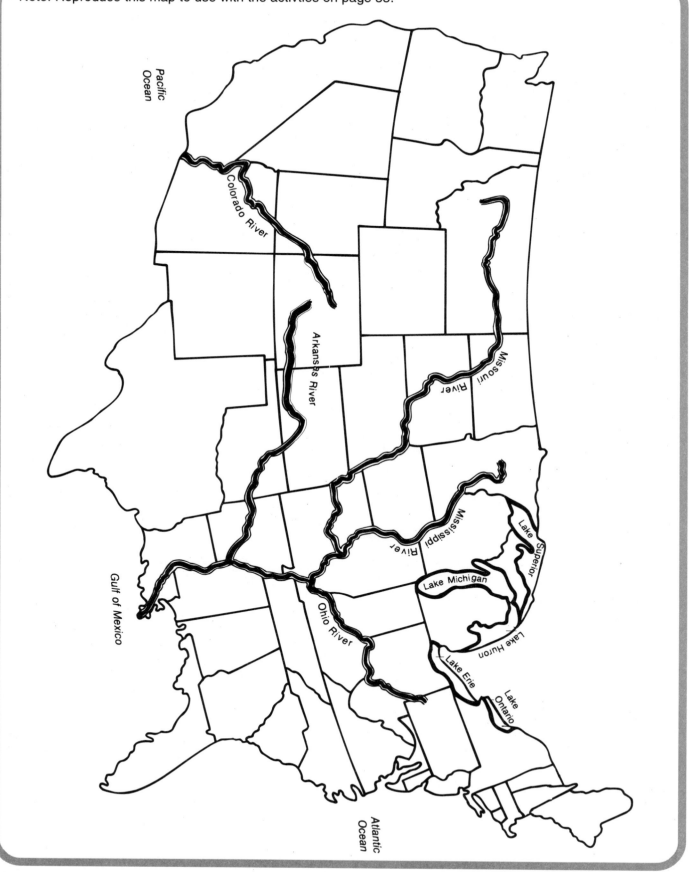

Note: Use the map on page 54 with these activities.

Oceans, Rivers, and Lakes

Use this map to introduce the major water ways in the United States. You may want to add other rivers and lakes that are appropriate before reproducing the map.

Oceans

Ask questions such as:

1. Which oceans touch the contiguous United States?

2. Which states touch the Pacific Ocean?

3. Which states touch the Atlantic Ocean?

Gulfs

Ask questions such as:

1. Which gulf is shown on this map?

2. How many states touch the Gulf of Mexico? Name them.

3. Which major U.S. river flows into the Gulf of Mexico?

Rivers

Ask questions such as:

1. Which rivers are shown on this map?

2. Are more states to the west or to the east of the Mississippi River?

3. Name the rivers that flow into the Mississippi River.

4. The (river name) flows through which states?

Lakes

Ask questions such as:

1. Name the Great Lakes.

2. Which of the Great Lakes has the same name as a state?

3. Which of the Great Lakes are partly in the United States and partly in Canada?

4. Name the U.S. states that touch one or more of the Great Lakes.

A River Journey

Have your students follow the steps below to plan a journey along one of the United States' major rivers.

1. Decide where your journey will begin and where it will end. Mark these spots on your map.

2. Trace your path with a marking pen or a crayon.

3. List all of the states through which you will pass on the back of your map. Draw a picture of the vehicle in which you will travel.

Note: Reproduce this map to use with the activities on page 57.

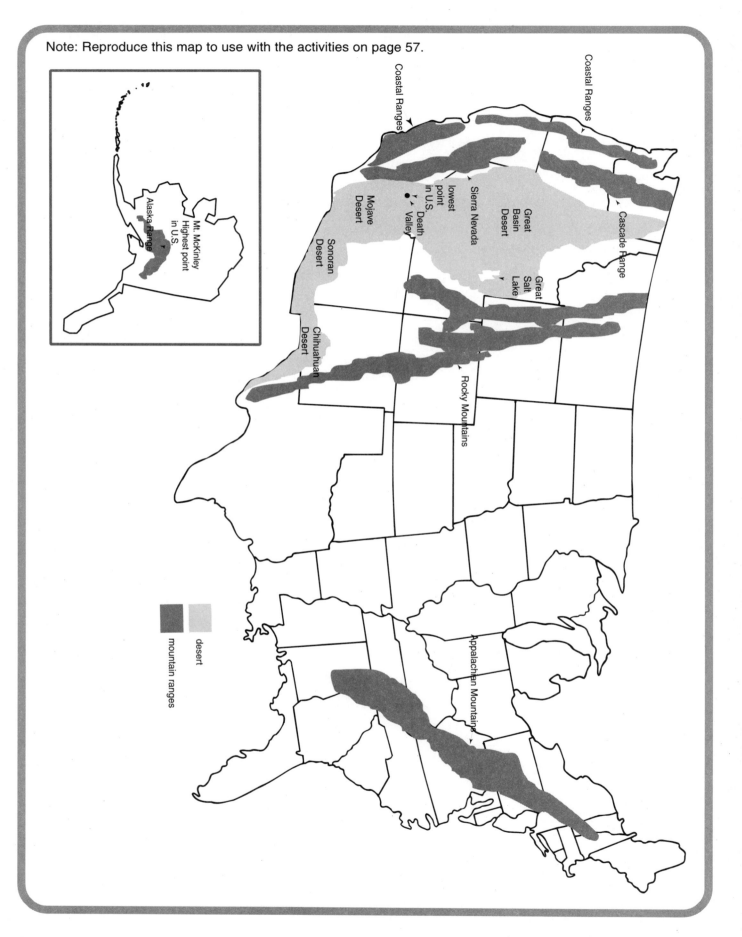

Coastal Ranges

Coastal Ranges

Mt. McKinley
Highest point
in U.S.

Alaska Range

Mojave
Desert

Sonoran
Desert

Chihuahuan
Desert

Death
Valley

lowest
point
in U.S.

Sierra Nevada

Great
Basin
Desert

Great
Salt
Lake

Cascade Range

Rocky Mountains

Appalachian Mountains

mountain ranges

desert

Note: Use the map on page 56 with these activities.

Major Mountain Ranges and Deserts

This map shows some of the many deserts and mountain ranges in the United States. You may wish to add others of specific interest to your unit of study before you reproduce the map for your students.

Mountain Ranges

Ask questions such as:

1. How many mountain ranges do you see on this map? Name them.

2. Are most of the mountain ranges shown in the western or eastern half of the United States?

3. Are more states east or west of the Rocky Mountains?

4. Which range of mountains is closest to where you live?

5. Which states would you pass through if you traveled from one end of the (name a mountain range) to the other?

6. In which state is the highest point in the United States located? What is the mountain called?

Deserts

Ask questions such as:

1. Which deserts do you see on this map?

2. Are most of the deserts shown west or east of the Rocky Mountains?

3. Are most of the deserts shown in the southwestern or northwestern part of the United States?

4. Which state has the largest percentage of its area covered in desert?

5. In which state is the lowest point in the United States located? What is it called?

Crossing the U.S.A.

Ask students to plan a route from New York to California following one of these sets of requirements. Mark the route with a crayon or a marking pen. (You may want students to plan more than one trip. Have them use a different color to represent each route.)

1. You have unlimited time, but you want to avoid as many mountain ranges and deserts as possible.

2. You want to come the shortest way possible, even if you must travel over mountains or through deserts.

3. You want to see as much of the Rocky Mountains as possible before you get to California.

4. You want to see both the Great Salt Lake and Death Valley on your trip.

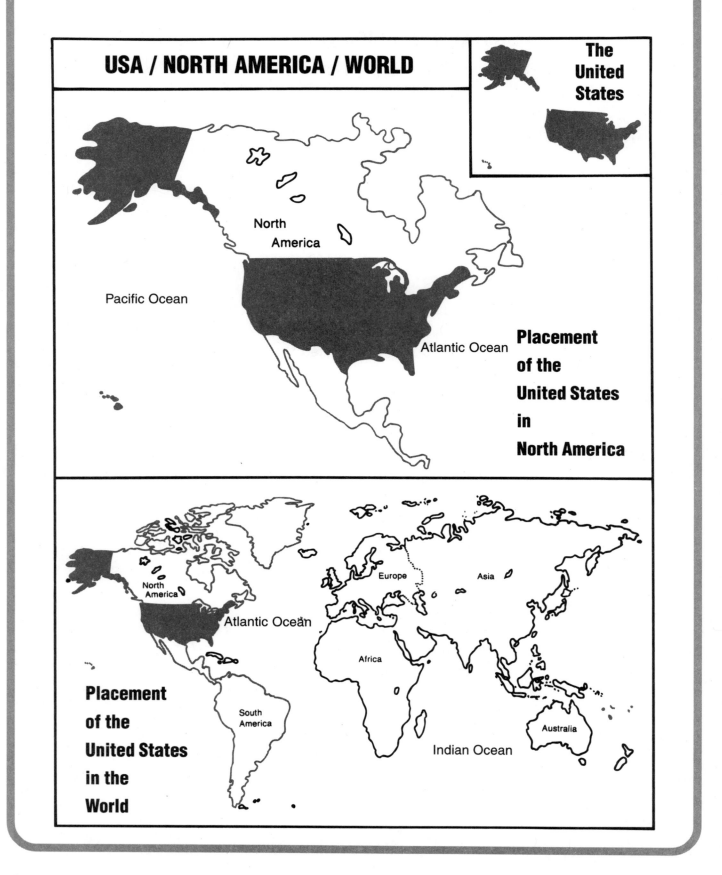

USA / NORTH AMERICA / WORLD

The United States

North America

Pacific Ocean

Atlantic Ocean

Placement of the United States in North America

North America

Atlantic Ocean

Europe

Asia

Africa

South America

Australia

Indian Ocean

Placement of the United States in the World

Maps of the U.S.A 1-6 EMC 191

U.S.A./North America/World

The dark areas on this map show the United States alone, its placement in North America, and its placement in relation to the rest of the world.

The United States of America

Touch each area and see if your students can name Alaska, the Hawaiian Islands, and the contingual United States.

North America

Ask questions such as:

1. What country would you go through while driving from Alaska to the rest of the United States?
2. In what ocean will you find the Hawaiian Islands?
3. Which two countries touch the United States?
4. What country is to the east of the Hawaiian Islands?
5. What country is to the north of the United States?
6. What country is to the south of the United States?

The World

Ask questions such as:

1. Is the United States in the eastern or western hemisphere?
2. Is the United States in the northern or southern hemisphere?
3. Which continent is south of North America?
4. If you travel east from the contigual United States, which two continents could you reach?
5. If you travel west from the contigual United States, which continent would you reach?

Add details to the map.

    a. Draw the equator on the world map.

    b. Write the names of other oceans, seas, and gulfs on the map.

    c. Plan a trip around the world that touches each of the continents shown on your map. Make a list telling your starting point and all the continents in the order you visit them.

Note: Reproduce this map to use with the activities on page 61.

Thirteen Original Colonies

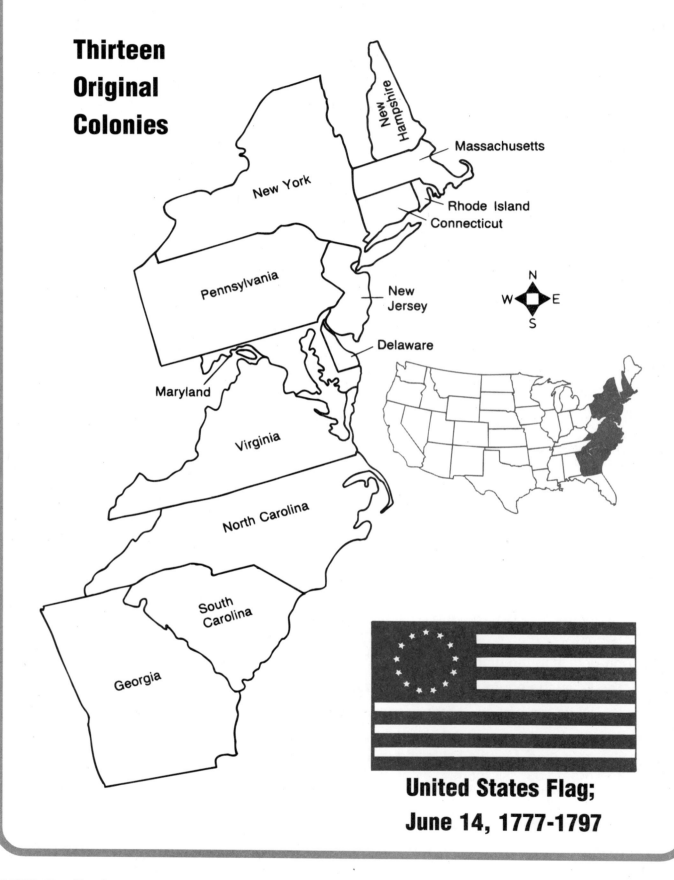

New Hampshire

New York

Massachusetts

Rhode Island

Connecticut

N
W E
S

Pennsylvania

New Jersey

Delaware

Maryland

Virginia

North Carolina

South Carolina

Georgia

United States Flag;
June 14, 1777-1797

Maps of the U.S.A 1-6 EMC 191

Note: Use the map on page 60 with these activities.

The Original Thirteen States

Map Study

Use this map as you ask questions about the size and position of the original thirteen states.

1. Which state is the smallest in area?

2. Which state is the farthest north?

3. Which of the original states did NOT touch the Atlantic Ocean?

4. Which of these states touch the border of Canada?

5. Which states would you pass through going from Rhode Island to Pennsylvania?

Admission to the Union

Use the information on the individual state maps to find the order in which the colonies became states. On the map write the admission date on each state. Then make a list of the states' names in the order they were admitted to the union.

Revolutionary War

Use the map as part of a study of the Revolutionary War.

- Mark important battlefields.

- Enlarge the map using an opaque or overhead projector. Display it in the classroom. Have students add city names, rivers, battlefields, etc. that were important during that period of history.

First Flag

Assign individual or small groups of students to find the answers to questions such as these about the first U.S. flag.

1. What is the meaning of the stars?

2. What do the stripes represent?

3. Why have the number of stars changed, but the thirteen stripes remained?

Time Zones

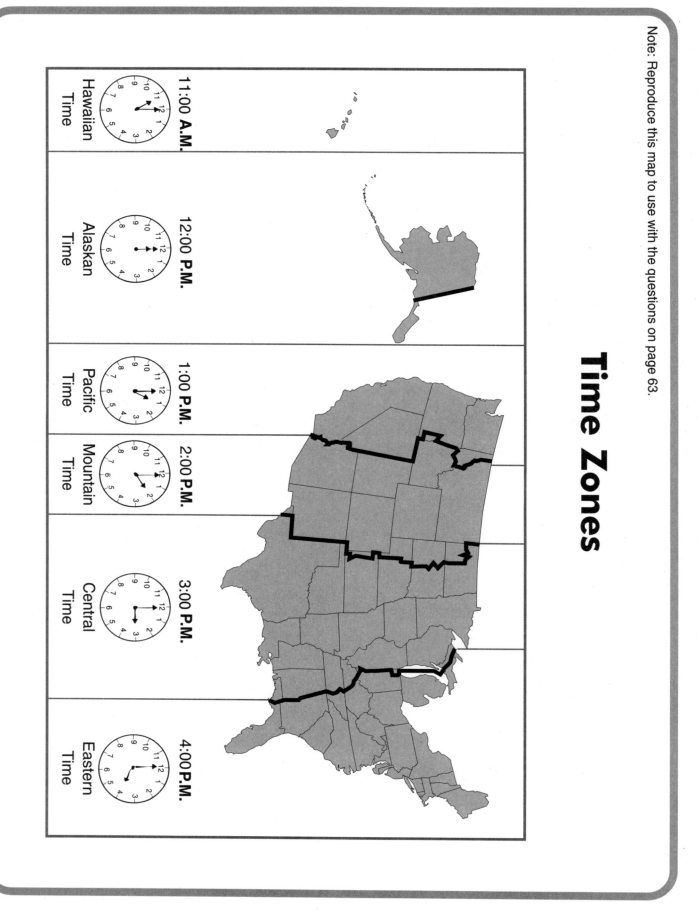

11:00 A.M.	12:00 P.M.	1:00 P.M.	2:00 P.M.	3:00 P.M.	4:00 P.M.
Hawaiian Time	Alaskan Time	Pacific Time	Mountain Time	Central Time	Eastern Time

Maps of the U.S.A 1-6 EMC 191

Note: Use with the map on page 62.

Time Zones

Find the Time Zones

Ask questions such as:

1. How many time zones do you see on this map? Name them.

2. How many hours difference is there between each time zone?

3. How many time zones would you cross going from the east coast to California?

4. Find Texas on your map. Which time zone/zones is it in?

5. Is your home state in one or more time zones?

6. Name the time zone in which you live.

What time is it?

Ask students to calculate changes in time.

1. If it is (name a time) in (name a state), what time will it be in...

   Alaska _____   California _____   Florida _____   Michigan _____

2. If it is 3 p.m. Central Time will it be earlier or later in the Pacific Time zone? How many hours difference will there be?

3. Harry lives in Hawaii. He called his grandmother in Florida. If he called at 2:15 p.m., what time was it at his grandmother's?

Challenge

Challenge students to each make up a word problem about time zones.
Have them write the question on a 3" x 5" card and the answer on the back.
Place the completed cards in a free-time center to see if classmates can solve each others' questions.

Answer Key

Alabama
★Montgomery
1. Alabama River
2. Coosa River
3. Tombigbee River
4. Birmingham
5. Mobile

Alaska
★Juneau
1. Yukon River
2. Kuskokwim River
3. Tanana River
4. Anchorage
5. Fairbanks

Arizona
★Phoenix
1. Colorado River
2. Little Colorado
3. Gila River
4. Scottsdale
5. Tucson
6. Yuma
7. Flagstaff

Arkansas
★Little Rock
1. Mississippi River
2. Arkansas River
3. White River
4. Hot Springs
5. Fayetteville
6. Texarkana

California
★Sacramento
1. Colorado River
2. San Joaquin River
3. Sacramento River
4. Eel River
5. San Francisco
6. Los Angeles
7. San Diego
8. Fresno

Colorado
★Denver
1. Colorado River
2. South Platte River
3. Arkansas River
4. Grand Junction
5. Boulder
6. Aspen
7. Greeley

Connecticut
★Hartford
1. Connecticut River
2. Housatonic River
3. New Haven
4. Bridgeport
5. Danbury

Delaware
★Dover
1. Delaware Bay
2. Delaware River
3. Newark
4. Seaford
5. Georgetown
6. Lewes

Florida
★Tallahassee
1. Lake Okeechobee
2. Kissimmee River
3. St. Johns River
4. Suwanee River
5. Pensacola
6. St. Petersburg
7. Miami
8. Jacksonville

Georgia
★Atlanta
1. Savannah River
2. Altamaha River
3. Chattahoochee River
4. Macon
5. Savannah
6. Augusta

Hawaii
★Honolulu
1. Niihau
2. Kauai
3. Oahu
4. Molokai
5. Lanai
6. Maui
7. Kahoolawe
8. Hawaii
9. Kona
10. Hilo
11. Hana
12. Lahaina

Idaho
★Boise
1. Snake River
2. Salmon River
3. Twin Falls
4. Pocatello
5. Coeur d' Alene

Illinois
★Springfield
1. Illinois River
2. Mississippi River
3. Wabash River
4. Carbondale
5. Chicago
6. Peoria
7. Waukegan

Indiana
★Indianapolis
1. Wabash River
2. Ohio River
3. Fort Wayne
4. Muncie
5. Evansville
6. Terre Haute

Iowa
★Des Moines
1. Des Moines River
2. Skunk River
3. Mississippi River
4. Council Bluffs
5. Sioux City
6. Cedar Rapids
7. Dubuque

Kansas
★Topeka
1. Arkansas River
2. Smoky Hill River
3. Kansas River
4. Wichita
5. Dodge City
6. Kansas City

Kentucky
★Frankfort
1. Ohio River
2. Kentucky River
3. Cumberland River
4. Louisville
5. Bowling Green
6. Paducah

Louisiana
★Baton Rouge
1. Lake Pontchartrain
2. Mississippi River
3. Red River
4. New Orleans
5. Shreveport
6. Alexandria

Maine
★Augusta
1. Kennebec River
2. Penobscot River
3. Portland
4. Brunswick
5. Bangor
6. Eastport

Maryland
★Annapolis
1. Potomac River
2. Patuxent River
3. Chesapeake Bay
4. Cumberland
5. Baltimore
6. Washington, D.C.

Massachusetts
★Boston
1. Connecticut River
2. Pittsfield
3. Nantucket Sound
4. Salem
5. Provincetown
6. Plymouth
7. Holyoke

Michigan
★Lansing
1. Grand River
2. Muskegon River
3. Lake Michigan
4. Flint
5. Detroit
6. Sault Ste. Marie

Minnesota
★Saint Paul
1. Mississippi River
2. Minnesota River
3. St. Croix River
4. Minneapolis
5. Duluth
6. Rochester

Mississippi
★Jackson
1. Pearl River
2. Yazoo River
3. Mississippi River
4. Vicksburg
5. Natchez
6. Meridian
7. Tupelo

Missouri
★Jefferson City
1. Mississippi River
2. Missouri River
3. Osage River
4. Branson
5. Kansas City
6. Independence
7. Hannibal

Montana
★Helena
1. Missouri River
2. Yellowstone River
3. Milk River
4. Butte
5. Bozeman
6. Billings

Nebraska
★Lincoln
1. Platte River
2. North Platte River
3. South Platte River
4. Niobrara River
5. North Platte
6. Omaha

Nevada
★Carson City
1. Humboldt River
2. Truckee River
3. Colorado River
4. Las Vegas
5. Reno
6. Virginia City
7. Winnemucca

New Hampshire
★Concord
1. Merrimack River
2. Connecticut River
3. Lake Winnipesaukee
4. Dover
5. Portsmouth
6. Nashua

New Jersey
★Trenton
1. Delaware River
2. Atlantic City
3. Princeton
4. Newark

New Mexico
★Santa Fe
1. Rio Grande
2. Pecos River
3. Canadian River
4. Las Cruces
5. Carlsbad
6. Gallup
7. Albuquerque

New York
★Albany
1. Hudson River
2. Mohawk River
3. Susquehanna River
4. New York City
5. Buffalo
6. Schenectady
7. Rochester

North Carolina
★Raleigh
1. Cape Fear River
2. Pamlico Sound
3. Winston-Salem
4. Charlotte
5. Greensboro

North Dakota
★Bismarck
1. Missouri River
2. Little Missouri River
3. Sheyenne River
4. James River
5. Fargo
6. Grand Forks

Ohio
★Columbus
1. Ohio River
2. Scioto River
3. Muskingum River
4. Cincinnati
5. Akron
6. Cleveland
7. Dayton

Oklahoma
★Oklahoma City
1. Red River
2. Canadian River
3. Arkansas River
4. Tulsa
5. Muskogee
6. Norman